P9-DCV-025

IRAN

Big Buddy Books
An Imprint of Abdo Publishing
abdopublishing.com

Julie Murray

EXPLORE THE COUNTRIES

abdopublishing.com

Published by Abdo Publishing, a division of ABDO, PO Box 398166, Minneapolis, Minnesota 55439.
Copyright © 2016 by Abdo Consulting Group, Inc. International copyrights reserved in all countries. No part of this book may be reproduced in any form without written permission from the publisher. Big Buddy Books™ is a trademark and logo of Abdo Publishing.

Printed in the United States of America, North Mankato, Minnesota.
092015
012016

Cover Photo: Shutterstock.com.
Interior Photos: ASSOCIATED PRESS (p. 19); Tim Gerard Barker/Getty Images (p. 35); Daniel Bockwoldt/picture-alliance/dpa/AP Images (p. 19); ANDREJ ISAKOVIC/AFP/Getty Images (p. 17); © iStockphoto.com (pp. 23, 35); Izzet Keribar/Getty Images (p. 34); Francois Lochon/Getty Images (p. 17); BEHROUZ MEHRI/AFP/Getty Images (p. 29); Photoshot/Getty Images (p. 31); Shutterstock.com (pp. 5, 9, 11, 13, 19, 21, 23, 25, 27, 34, 35, 37, 38); Stock Montage/Getty Images (p. 16); ullstein bild/Getty Images (p. 15); The Washington Post/Getty Images (p. 33).

Coordinating Series Editor: Megan M. Gunderson
Editor: Katie Lajiness
Contributing Editors: Bridget O'Brien, Marcia Zappa
Graphic Design: Adam Craven

Country population and area figures taken from the CIA World Factbook.

Library of Congress Cataloging-in-Publication Data

Murray, Julie, 1969-
Iran / Julie Murray.
    pages cm. -- (Explore the countries)
Includes index.
ISBN 978-1-68078-067-3
1. Iran--Juvenile literature. I. Title.
DS254.75.M87 2016
955--dc23

2015025164

IRAN

CONTENTS

AROUND THE WORLD

Our world has many countries. Each country has beautiful land. It has its own rich history. And, the people have their own languages and ways of life.

Iran is a country in Asia. What do you know about Iran? Let's learn more about this place and its story!

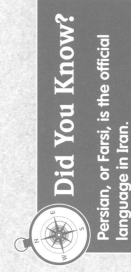

Did You Know?

Persian, or Farsi, is the official language in Iran.

4

In Kandovan, people live in cone-shaped caves. Flowing water wore down rocks to form these special shapes.

5

Passport to Iran

Iran is located in a part of the world known as the Middle East. Seven countries border Iran. In addition, the Caspian Sea is to the north. The Gulf of Oman and the Persian Gulf are to the south.

Iran's total area is 636,372 square miles (1,648,195 sq km). More than 81.8 million people live there.

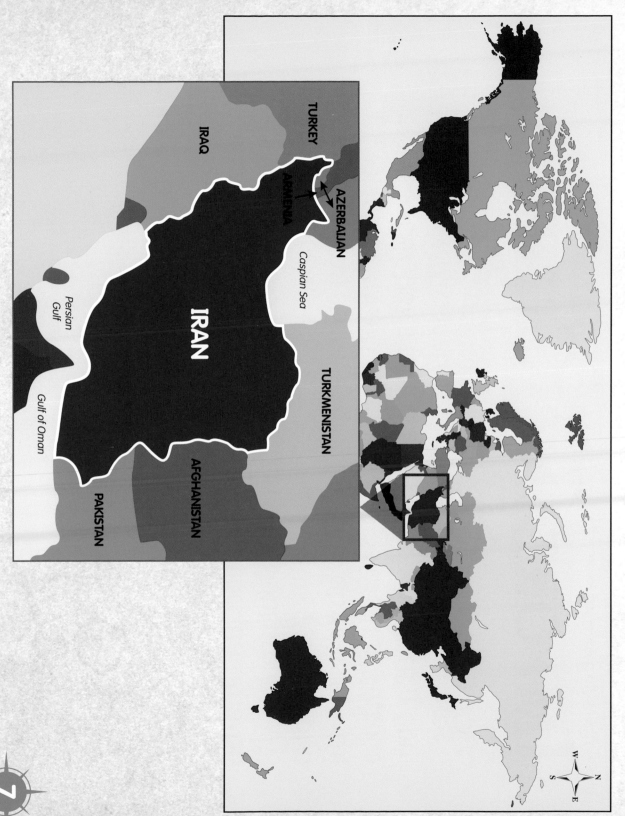

TURKEY

IRAQ

ARMENIA

AZERBAIJAN

Caspian Sea

IRAN

TURKMENISTAN

Persian
Gulf

Gulf of Oman

AFGHANISTAN

PAKISTAN

IMPORTANT CITIES

Tehran is Iran's **capital** and largest city, with more than 8 million people. This city looks very modern. New construction projects help the city grow. For easier travel in a large city, people ride public trains and buses.

Many mosques are near shopping centers and government buildings. A mosque is a building where *Muslims* pray.

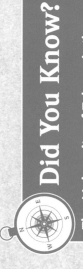

Did You Know?

The University of Tehran is the largest school in Iran. More than 35,000 students attend every year.

SAY IT

Tehran
tay-RAN

mosque
MAHSK

Milad Tower is the highest building in Tehran. It is more than 1,000 feet (305 m) tall!

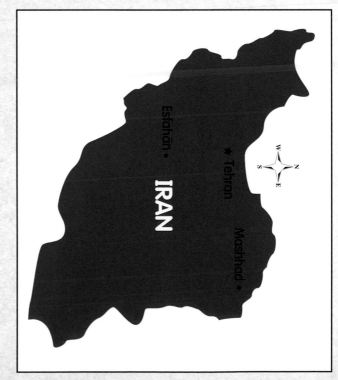

IRAN

Eşfahān •

★ Tehran •

Mashhad •

N
W   E
S

Mashhad is Iran's second-largest city with about 2.7 million people. This city is laid out in a circle. Faith-based monuments are in the center. Mashhad's major business is natural gas. This kind of gas is often used for heating and cooking. Esfahān is Iran's third-largest city. More than 1.7 million people live there. Highways and air travel help people go from Esfahān to Tehran. Esfahān is known for steel manufacturing.

Mashhad is known for producing fruits, nuts, and wool. Many of its goods are sold in busy shopping centers called bazaars.

SAY IT

bazaar
buh-ZAHR

Esfahān is famous for its beautiful woven rugs.

Iran in History

People have lived in what is now Iran for thousands of years. **Aryan**, or Irani, tribes traveled to the area around 1500 BC. They called their new home *Irania*. But, it became known around the world as Persia.

Persian kings ruled southwestern Asia and parts of Europe and Africa. **Arabs** overcame present-day Iran in the AD mid-600s. Many people became **Muslims**. By the mid-800s, the area that is now Iran was a major center for art and science.

12

Persepolis was a city in ancient Persia. It was built in about 500 B.C. Parts of the city's buildings are still standing in Iran today.

13

Persia had a long history of fighting over land and society. Between 1804 and 1828, Persia lost two wars with Russia.

In 1906, a modern government was created in what is now Iran. The next five years of struggle are known as the Constitutional Revolution. This was a fight over the government and its rules.

The **Islamic** Revolution took place from 1978 to 1979. Ruhollah Khomeini was an important **Muslim** leader also known as an ayatollah. He took the government away from the shah, or king. Then, Iran became an Islamic republic.

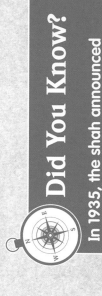

Did You Know?

In 1935, the shah announced Persia would be called by its ancient name, Iran.

Khomeini ruled Iran from 1979 to 1989.

SAY IT

ayatollah
eye-uh-TOH-luh

Ruhollah Khomeini
ROO-hah-lee koh-MAY-nee

TIMELINE

About 550 BC

The Persian language was first written. It is read right to left.

1964

Khomeini was banned from Iran for disagreeing with the shah about Islam. He returned to Iran after the shah left the country. Many Iranians were happy when Khomeini became leader of Iran in 1979.

AD 1220

Mongol leader Genghis Khan took over what is now Iran. He controlled the area for many years. Under Mongol rule, many Iranian cities were destroyed. And, art and science declined.

1980–1988

Iraq and Iran fought over land between both countries. At least 1 million people were hurt or killed.

2003

In December, an earthquake hit the city of Bam. About 40,000 people lost their lives. Many countries sent supplies to help those in need.

2014

Five Iranians took part in the Winter Olympics. They appeared in alpine and cross-country ski races. They did not win any medals.

An Important Symbol

Iran's flag was adopted in 1980. It has three stripes. They are green, white, and red.

Iran's government is a **theocratic republic**. The country's supreme leader controls the government as well as the people's faith.

The president is the head of government. He serves a four-year term. Iran's president answers to the supreme leader, who is the head of state.

Iran is divided into 31 provinces. A province is a large section within a country, like a state.

In 2013, Hasan Ruhani was elected president of Iran.

Ayatollah Ali Khamenei became Iran's supreme leader in 1989. A supreme leader in the country rules for life.

Iran's flag has the Arabic words for "God is great" written 22 times along the edges of the stripes.

SAY IT

Ali Khamenei
ah-LEE kah-MAY-nay

Hasan Ruhani
ha-SAHN roo-AH-nee

Across the Land

Iran has mountains, deserts, coasts, islands, and plains. About 10 percent of Iran is forest. Oak, beech, walnut, and elm trees grow in these areas.

Iran has big weather changes. Summers in some areas are very hot. Temperatures can reach 130°F (54°C)! But, winters in most areas of Iran are cold.

Did You Know?

In January, Tehran's average temperature is 35°F (2°C). In July, it is 85°F (29°C).

Hormuz Island is off the southern coast of Iran. It does not have a lot of plant life. The island is mostly covered with rocks.

Many types of animals live in Iran. Seagulls, ducks, and geese are found near the Caspian Sea and Persian Gulf. Fish such as carp, catfish, sardines, sole, and tuna swim in their waters. Leopards, bears, and wild boars live in the wooded mountains.

Did You Know?

There are few green sea turtles left in the waters near Iran. Small populations face dirty waters and over-hunting of eggs and adults.

Iran is home to many types of lizards and snakes, such as vipers.

Gazelles live in Iran's wooded areas.

Earning a Living

Iran produces important goods. Oil, natural gas, and iron come from the ground. The country's factories make cars, tools, and foods. Iran's farms grow grains, nuts, and fruits. **Nomads** raise sheep and cattle. Fishing is common in the Persian Gulf and the Caspian Sea. Iran is famous for its caviar. This fancy food is made of fish eggs.

24

Iran is one of the world's largest growers of pistachio nuts.

LIFE IN IRAN

Iranian **culture** is one of the oldest in the Middle East. The country has a rich history with great art, food, and sports. It also has strong **religious traditions**. Poems have been popular in Iran for hundreds of years. Beautiful writing known as calligraphy is also common.

Iranian foods often have a lot of spices. Saffron is a popular spice used in many dishes. People in Iran eat a mix of fruits, nuts, and meats.

Did You Know?

In Iran, children must attend school from ages 6 to 11. The average person receives 15 years of education.

26

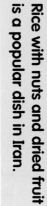

Rice with nuts and dried fruit is a popular dish in Iran.

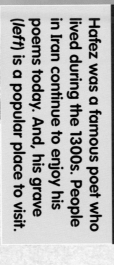

Hafez was a famous poet who lived during the 1300s. People in Iran continue to enjoy his poems today. And, his grave (left) is a popular place to visit.

Many people in Iran enjoy watching and playing sports. Soccer is popular in Iran. Horse racing, wrestling, and weight lifting are other common sports.

Nearly everyone in Iran is **Muslim**. Iran is the only country where Shia is the official state faith. Shia is the second-largest branch of **Islam**.

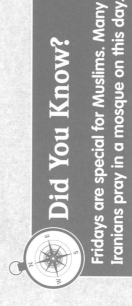

Did You Know?

Fridays are special for Muslims. Many Iranians pray in a mosque on this day.

Many people enjoy horse racing in Iran.

FAMOUS FACES

Many talented people are from Iran. Christiane Amanpour was born on January 12, 1958, in London, England. She moved to Tehran as a child. Amanpour became a famous reporter for the US television station CNN. She traveled the world to report the news.

SAY IT

Christiane Amanpour
KRIS-tee-ahn
Ah-MAHN-poor

Did You Know?

Amanpour's family left Iran in 1979. They moved to the United States.

In 2009, Amanpour began her own show on CNN. She talks about news happening all over the world.

Marjane Satrapi was born on November 22, 1969, in Rasht. She grew up in Tehran. Satrapi has written books and made films.

Satrapi is best known for her graphic novels. These books use cartoons to tell a story. *Persepolis 1–4* are about her life in Tehran and Europe. *Persepolis* became a film in 2007.

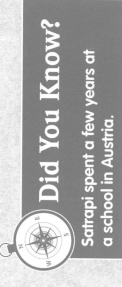

Did You Know?

Satrapi spent a few years at a school in Austria.

SAY IT

Marjane Satrapi
MAHR-jane
sah-TRAH-pee

Satrapi has won many awards for her books and films.

Tour Book

Imagine traveling to Iran! Here are some places you could go and things you could do.

Seek

Golestan Palace is believed to be one of Tehran's oldest castles. See the beautiful gardens and pools once owned by shahs.

Shop

Some areas of Tehran's Grand Bazaar are around 400 years old. Shop for carpets, spices, clothing, and so much more! Visitors can haggle, or argue, over goods to receive a fair price.

Learn

The Carpet Museum of Iran has many Persian carpets from all over the country. Some carpets are from the 1600s!

Discover

Eram Garden is one of the most famous Persian gardens in Iran. It is known for its pool and its tall trees.

Travel

Visitors can see remains of old buildings from ancient Persia. The city of Persepolis dates back to about 500 BC.

A GREAT COUNTRY

The story of Iran is important to our world. Iran is a land of vast deserts and beautiful mountains. It is a country of people with strong beliefs. The people and places that make up Iran offer something special. They help make the world a more beautiful, interesting place.

36

The Pink Mosque in Shiraz is known for its colorful tiles and stained glass windows.

Iran Up Close

Official Name: Islamic Republic of Iran

Flag:

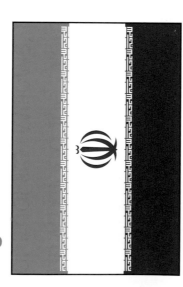

Population (rank): 81,824,270
(July 2015 est.)
(19th most-populated country)

Total Area (rank): 636,372 square miles
(18th largest country)

Capital: Tehran

Official Language: Persian

Currency: Iranian rial

Form of Government: Theocratic republic

National Anthem: "Soroud-e
Melli-ye Jomhouri-ye Eslami-ye Iran"
(National Anthem of the Islamic Republic
of Iran)

IMPORTANT WORDS

Arab of or relating to a member of the people who are originally from the Arabian Peninsula and who now live mostly in the Middle East and northern Africa. Something Arabian relates to Arab people or culture or the Arabic language.

Aryan (air-YEHN) a group of people who settled in ancient Iran.

capital a city where government leaders meet.

culture (KUHL-chuhr) the arts, beliefs, and ways of life of a group of people.

Islam a religion based on a belief in Allah as God and Muhammad as his prophet.

Muslim a person who practices Islam.

nomad a person who travels from place to place.

religious of or related to religion, which is the service and worship of God or the supernatural.

theocratic republic a form of government in which the leader is also a religious leader. Iran is an Islamic Republic.

tradition (truh-DIH-shuhn) a belief, a custom, or a story handed down from older people to younger people.

WEBSITES

To learn more about Explore the Countries, visit **booklinks.abdopublishing.com**. These links are routinely monitored and updated to provide the most current information available.

INDEX